Mary and the Ladies

A 12 Days of Christmas Devotional

Christina Clare

Cover art: *Madonna and Child with St. Catherine and St. Barbara* by Bernardino Luini (public domain)

Cover design: Rosemary Strohm

ISBN: 979-8-9903502-0-5 (paperback)

979-8-9903502-1-2 (hardcover)

979-8-9903502-2-9 (ebook)

Contents

Introduction

How to read this devotional:

One goal of this project is for the devotional to be used every year during the Christmas season. It is easy to get lost in the hustle and bustle of the holidays or to feel like everything is over once presents have been opened. This devotional is simple; my hope is that it can be a short moment you take for yourself to reflect on the season; on Mary, Joseph, and Jesus; and on you. While the devotional may be the same every year, you are not! How has life changed between this year and last year? What do you hope for the following year?

Each day begins with art of the Saint facing the Gospel reading of the day. The readings *almost* never change. Unfortunately, a few holidays rotate (at least in the United States), so if one of the readings seems different than the one at Mass that is why. All readings are from the Lectionary for Mass for Use in the Dioceses of the United States (second edition). This is followed by a biography of the saint(s) for the day with some reflection or prayer (for ease of readability I put the sources together in the end). It is also fine to do something else! Do you journal? Are you artistic? More meditative? Liturgical dancer? One benefit to this condensed devotional is that I leave it up to you how to spend this time with the Mary and the Ladies.

Well, ladies and Peter. This will make sense on December 29th.

The art for the 12 days have all been commissioned for this project specifically and completed by 12 different women. Because of the wonderful backers who supported the kickstarter campaign there is a bonus day, Christmas Eve, and the reproduction of Kristyn Brown's "Morning Star."

Most of all I hope this brings you a few moments of peace in this beautiful season.

Christmas Eve

H oly Mother,

As we wait with you this evening we give you thanks for the gift we are about to receive.

Mary, most faithful servant, may we model your steadfast love. Teach us to say 'yes' to God and to love your son more fully.

December 25

Luke 2: 1-14 Night Mass

I n those days a decree went out from Caesar Augustus
 that the whole world should be enrolled.
This was the first enrollment,
when Quirinius was governor of Syria.
So all went to be enrolled, each to his own town.
And Joseph too went up from Galilee from the town of Nazareth
to Judea, to the city of David that is called Bethlehem,
because he was of the house and family of David,
to be enrolled with Mary, his betrothed, who was with child.
While they were there,
the time came for her to have her child,
and she gave birth to her firstborn son.
She wrapped him in swaddling clothes and laid him in a manger,
because there was no room for them in the inn.
    Now there were shepherds in that region living in the fields
and keeping the night watch over their flock.
The angel of the Lord appeared to them
and the glory of the Lord shone around them,
and they were struck with great fear.
The angel said to them,
"Do not be afraid;
for behold, I proclaim to you good news of great joy
that will be for all the people.
For today in the city of David
a savior has been born for you who is Christ and Lord.
And this will be a sign for you:
you will find an infant wrapped in swaddling clothes
and lying in a manger."
And suddenly there was a multitude of the heavenly host with the angel,
praising God and saying:
    "Glory to God in the highest
    and on earth peace to those on whom his favor rests."

St. Anastasia

d. 304

M ost of what we know of Anastasia comes from legend and the lives of contemporary male saints. What we do know is she is named in the Canon of the Mass, the Sacramentary of St. Gregory, and other lists of martyrs of the Early Church. She is commemorated in the second Mass on Christmas Day and is only one of seven women commemorated in the Roman Canon of the Mass . A Church in Rome is dedicated to God in memory of Anastasia.

According to legend, she was from a well-to-do Roman family who were also early Roman martyrs. She was taught by St. Chrysogonus, and when he was persecuted under Emperor Dioclesian she went to visit him in prison. Legend tells us she traveled to care for imprisoned Christians, tending their wounds. This included those suffering from poisoning, which is how she came to be known as "Deliverer from Potions." While caring for others, she was caught and the authorities realized she was a Christian. Anastasia was sentenced to be burned alive in 304 in Sirmium. Her remains were brought to Rome to be buried in the church built in her name before they were lost in the invasion of the Turks. While her remains have disappeared the church is still there. Anastasia is the patron saint of martyrs, weavers, and those suffering from poison.

It seems odd to think of a woman's death (and horrific death at that) on such a joyous day. It is a stark reminder that the birth of Christ has meaning because of his death that we commemorate each year with the Paschal Triduum. Without the death and resurrection of Jesus, His birth would have been like that of any regular child to a single mother. Because we have the Resurrection, though, we commemorate so many individuals like Anastasia who were brave enough to give their lives for the Truth. As we celebrate the Nativity (with presents and good food—like every birthday!) it is an excellent time to reflect on the gift we receive from Jesus himself.

What jumps out to you, either from the Gospel reading or about Saint Anastasia? Is there a 'poison' is in your spiritual life? This might be a weird question to ask on Christmas, but while caught up in the joy of Jesus' birth, is there something you wish to change in your spiritual life? Perhaps you have made progress in the past year; now is an excellent time to ponder and celebrate that!

Saint Anastasia, today we celebrate the birth of our Savior, Christ the Lord. Help me to announce his salvation through my deeds. Lift my heart to tend to others as you did.

St. Vincenta
María López y
Vicuña

December 26

Matthew 10: 17-22

J esus said to his disciples:
"Beware of men, for they will hand you over to courts
and scourge you in their synagogues,
and you will be led before governors and kings for my sake
as a witness before them and the pagans.
When they hand you over,
do not worry about how you are to speak
or what you are to say.
You will be given at that moment what you are to say.
For it will not be you who speak
but the Spirit of your Father speaking through you.
Brother will hand over brother to death,
and the father his child;
children will rise up against parents and have them put to death.
You will be hated by all because of my name,
but whoever endures to the end will be saved."

St. Vicenta Maria Lopez Y Vicuna

1847-1896

St. Vicenta was born on March 22, 1847, in Cascante, Spain. Her parents began her education early, and she demonstrated an aptitude for teaching and learning. She went to Madrid to continue her education and lived with her aunt, Eulolia de Vicuna. While she lived with her aunt, she was moved by her aunt's charity—Eulolia had created a home for domestic servants. Vicenta decided to model herself after Eulolia and took a vow of chastity. The two organized a group of like-minded women to minister to working girls. She wrote a written rule and, with three others, took religious vows. This was the beginning of the Daughters of Mary Immaculate for Domestic Service, which would receive papal approbation in 1888.

Vicenta died on December 26, 1890 in Madrid. She was first named Venerable on March 21, 1943, by Pope Pius XII who proclaimed she lived a life of heroic virtue. He later Beatified Vicenta on February 19, 1950. Pope Paul VI canonized her in 1975, citing how her dedication to the service of others reflected the depths of devotion and care that Joseph and Mary exemplified.

Vicenta saw a group in a rapidly changing society that was being neglected: working women. The industrial revolution was taking on steam in Europe, leading to many social and economic changes. Life for working women outside the home has always been challenging, and Vicenta became a type of foster mother for the domestic servants, her congregation providing a voice at a time there were virtually no protections for workers. Ann Ball writes of Vicenta as having the gift of seeing each person as an individual and recognizing their true value before God. She respected and loved them and was eager to give them what they needed in order to make the most of themselves. She treated each girl as her own daughter.

Today the congregation is present on 4 continents, still working with the youth.

Saint Vicenta witnessed the rapid changes the Industrial Revolution brought to her society. There are many exciting changes (and growth!) industrializing brings, but not everyone benefits. Who is left out of society (and/or the economy) today? Jesus spent his earthly ministry tending to the outcasts in society, something Saint Vicenta's work reflects. Many hands make like work; is there a community of like-minded individuals doing the work I feel called to? Am I being called to start such a community?

Some big questions for the day after Christmas! This is not meant to overwhelm, it is simply how Saint Vicenta speaks to me at this moment in my life. Is there something from her life that speaks to you? Does something from the Gospel stand out?

The Lord is my rock and my fortress, and I will rejoice and be glad in His Mercy. St. Vicenta, you witnessed so much change in your community and reached out to those most in need of Mercy. Help me identify those who are most in need of help that I may be of service to them as you were.

December 27

John 20: 1-8

On the first day of the week,
  Mary Magdalene ran and went to Simon Peter
and to the other disciple whom Jesus loved, and told them,
"They have taken the Lord from the tomb,
and we do not know where they put him."
So Peter and the other disciple went out and came to the tomb.
They both ran, but the other disciple ran faster than Peter
and arrived at the tomb first;
he bent down and saw the burial cloths there, but did not go in.
When Simon Peter arrived after him,
he went into the tomb and saw the burial cloths there,
and the cloth that had covered his head,
not with the burial cloths but rolled up in a separate place.
Then the other disciple also went in,
the one who had arrived at the tomb first,
and he saw and believed.

St. Fabiola

d. 399

S everal sources write how Fabiola, a Roman woman of rank born in the fourth century, divorced her violent husband according to Roman law but married her second husband before her first died. This was against the teachings of the Church, and she feared this sin led to her second husband dying young. When her second husband passed (in some accounts soon after their marriage), she returned to the Lateran Basilica dressed in penitential garb to repent for this sin, a display that even the Pope remarked on. She dedicated the remainder of her life to asceticism and nursing others.

She was one of fifteen women disciples of St. Jerome, most likely adopting Christian asceticism from him. In the span of a few short years, she helped to build several hospitals. First in 395, she lived and worked in a hospice in Bethlehem with Saint Paula. She returned to Rome and helped to build a hospital for pilgrims. She then worked with Saint Pammachius to build a hospital in Porto Romano.

Fabiola's contemporaries, and later scholars, refer to her as a physician. Marilyn Bailey Ogilvie writes that she was pragmatic rather than theoretical (a critique I find harsh for the fourth century) in her medical skills. She was renowned for helping, as St. Jerome described them, "rejects from society who suffered from loathsome diseases."

Fabiola died in 399 and received a funeral service that demonstrated the gratitude and veneration the people had for her. Her legacy lived on. Cardinal Wiseman wrote a novelized version of her life in 1854 to combat the popular Protestant novel *Hypatia* during a time when British Catholics were beginning to be allowed to practice their faith openly. In 1885, French artist Jean-Jacques Henner created a famous portrait of Fabiola with her face turned left and she wore a red scarf. The portrait has disappeared, but today Belgian artist Francis Alÿs has created a gallery of over 450 reproductions from around the world of the portrait, *Francis Alÿs: The Fabiola Project.*

Paired with the Gospel reading, the Psalm asks us to rejoice and reminds us that God's kingdom is one of justice (some version of the word appears eight times in the Responsorial Psalm). Fabiola shows that we are his representatives on earth, so our works should bring justice to those around us. During one Easter sermon, the line that stuck with me all these years later (over a decade at this point) was that because of Jesus's resurrection, everything changed. We do good works not because we have to, but because when we believe in the power of the Resurrection it changes something inside us to want to do good in the world. It might seem weird to reflect on a homily from Easter at Christmas, but the birth of Christ is celebrated because of the resurrection. We are celebrating *because* everything has changed!

I do wonder about some of the events of Fabiola's life. Was she motived out of fear for her sins? At what point did her motivation change? Did she find joy in serving others? In what ways can I serve those around me to create a more just world? Of all the Saints in all the world, why were people obsessed with one portrait with a red scarf? (Okay, not Christmas related but this is such a random nugget of information!)

Saint Fabiola, pray for us!

December 28

Matthew 2: 13-18

W hen the magi had departed, behold,
the angel of the Lord appeared to Joseph in a dream and said,
"Rise, take the child and his mother, flee to Egypt,
and stay there until I tell you.
Herod is going to search for the child to destroy him."
Joseph rose and took the child and his mother by night
and departed for Egypt.
He stayed there until the death of Herod,
that what the Lord had said through the prophet might be fulfilled,
Out of Egypt I called my son.

When Herod realized that he had been deceived by the magi,
he became furious.
He ordered the massacre of all the boys in Bethlehem and its vicinity
two years old and under,
in accordance with the time he had ascertained from the magi.
Then was fulfilled what had been said through Jeremiah the prophet:

A voice was heard in Ramah,
sobbing and loud lamentation;
Rachel weeping for her children,
and she would not be consoled,
since they were no more.

St. Caterina Volpicelli

1839-1894

Born on January 21, 1839 to an upper middle class family, Caterina was a well-educated girl. The Vatican writes she wanted to 'outshine' her sister in society and tried to be a socialite. She eventually heeded the call to adhere to a holy vocation. She had a chance meeting with Bl. Ludovicoda Casoria on September 19, 1854 in Naples, which led to Caterina joining the Third Order Franciscans. This would introduce her to the devotion to the Sacred Heart of Jesus, which soon became her life's goal. She first tried to join the Congregation of Perpetual Adorers but was rejected due to her health. While she suffered from physical ailments, her desire to create an apostolic life was strong. She longed to "revive love for Jesus Christ in hearts, in families, and in society" which led to, first, Caterina joining the Apostleship of Prayer and, eventually, in July 1874, created the new institute Servants of the Sacred Heart. This would receive Papal appropriation on June 13, 1890. She led the efforts to open several orphanages throughout Italy and the order was also known for tending to cholera victims. Caterina attended the first National Eucharistic Congress celebrated in Naples in 1891. She died in Naples on December 28, 1894.

Caterina was canonized by Pope Benedict XVI on April 26, 2009. During the Mass, Pope Benedict said Caterina was "a witness of divine love, in a period of spiritual and social crisis. For her, the secret was the Eucharist." We are called, he added, to a conversion that radically changes the heart, and that requires we "release God from the prisons in which human beings have confined him." Thus, it is possible to "lay the foundations for building a society open to justice and solidarity, overcoming that economic and cultural imbalance which continues to exist in a large part of our planet."

Caterina was another saint witnessing enormous social and economic changes in her time. The Responsorial Psalm (124) feels appropriate for Caterina. She tried to live her life in an earthly way, as was expected of her station. Only after she breaks away from earthly temptations does she find true joy and fulfillment as well as service to others. I am drawn to the part of today's Psalm, "Broken was the Snare, and we were freed."

Is there part of the Gospel that speaks to you today? What line comes to mind first?

I have reached a place in myself where I don't compare myself to my siblings or my closest friends—who has the better house? Am I achieving the 'goals' society says I should be? This is not a brag—I struggle in other areas of materialism. Are there areas you struggle with? It is easy to get absorbed with the commercialism of the season, what does life look like on an average day in May or September?

Saint Caterina, you lost yourself to Jesus' Sacred Heart and in so doing found a love so profound and fulfilling. I pray, help me find that divine love in my life that I may reflect it back to others around me.

December 29

Luke 2: 22-35

When the days were completed for their purification
according to the law of Moses,
the parents of Jesus took him up to Jerusalem
to present him to the Lord,
just as it is written in the law of the Lord,
Every male that opens the womb shall be consecrated to the Lord,
and to offer the sacrifice of
a pair of turtledoves or two young pigeons,
in accordance with the dictate in the law of the Lord.
　　Now there was a man in Jerusalem whose name was Simeon.
This man was righteous and devout,
awaiting the consolation of Israel,
and the Holy Spirit was upon him.
It had been revealed to him by the Holy Spirit
that he should not see death
before he had seen the Christ of the Lord.
He came in the Spirit into the temple;
and when the parents brought in the child Jesus
to perform the custom of the law in regard to him,
he took him into his arms and blessed God, saying:
　　"Lord, now let your servant go in peace;
your word has been fulfilled:
my own eyes have seen the salvation
which you prepared in the sight of every people,
a light to reveal you to the nations
and the glory of your people Israel."
　　The child's father and mother were amazed at what was said about him;
and Simeon blessed them and said to Mary his mother,
"Behold, this child is destined
for the fall and rise of many in Israel,
and to be a sign that will be contradicted
(and you yourself a sword will pierce)
so that the thoughts of many hearts may be revealed."

Martyrs of Seoul

1839

O n this day, the Church recognizes seven martyrs—six women and one man—who were beheaded in 1839 outside the small west gate, the ancient city wall built at the end of the fourteenth century.

Ko Sun-I "Barbara" was born in Seoul in 1794 and married Pak Augustine at 18. They had three children, and the entire family engaged in charitable work and helped care for the sick. Both Barbara and her husband were arrested for being Catholic. After two months in prison, Barbara was martyred at the age of 42.

Yi Yŏng-dŏk "Magdalene" was the older sister of Yi In-dŏk Mary. She was born in 1811 to a noble but poor family. Her grandmother taught her the Catholic faith and she, her sister, and their mother converted to Catholicism. Her father was anti-Catholic and arranged a marriage for her to a non-Catholic. Eventually Magdalene, her sister, and their mother escaped to a friendly Catholic home in Seoul before they were arrested. Magdalene witnessed her mother die in prison before she herself was martyred at the age of 28.

Chŏng Chŏng-hye "Elizabeth" was born to a Catholic family. Her parents and brother were martyrs of the faith. She used her skills of sewing to provide for her family. She was well respected for her piety and dedication to the Catholic community, even while in prison. She was martyred at the age of 43.

Cho Chŭng-i "Barbara" was born in 1781 to a renowned family and married young to Nam I-gwan "Sebastian". She gave birth to a son who died shortly after being born. After her husband was sent into exile in 1801, she moved to Seoul to live with a devout Catholic family. She would be able to help with foreign missionaries who arrived in Korea including housing several fathers and Bishop Imbert. She was arrested in July and would be martyred at the age of 58.

Ch'oe Ch'ang-hŭb "Peter" was born in 1786, and his father was a government official. His father passed away when he was 13, and then his older brother was martyred in 1801. He did not become active in the Catholic community until several years later when he met his future wife Son Magdalene. They would have eleven children, only two of whom survived childhood. He was arrested with his wife and one daughter. He was martyred at the age of 53.

Han Yŏng-i "Magdalene" married Kwŏn Chin who was a scholarly government official from a noble family. Kwŏn converted first when he reached middle age, and he asked Magdalene to convert. On his deathbed, he asked Magdalene to continue to live as a Catholic. She lived with her daughter and her daughter's friend, both Catholic, for several years before all three were arrested for being Catholic. She was martyred at 56 years old.

Hyŏn Kyŏng-nyŏn "Benedicta" was from a Catholic family. Her father and father-in-law were both martyred in 1801 and her sister would be martyred in 1846. She married in 1811 but her husband died three years later before they could have children. She dedicated her life to prayer, meditation, and spiritual reading. She was admired for her pious life. She would be arrested in July before being martyred at the age of 46.

The Gospel reading for today is usually Luke 2:22-35 (occasionally it is the passage immediately after when Mary and Joseph lose Jesus in the Temple). The focus is on Jesus fulfilling the prophecies of the Old Testament and on community. Community is a theme that came to mind while researching these Martyrs. A community of like-minded believers had to have made life easier in difficult and dark times as Catholics hid their faith. It also had to provide some comfort (I hope) while they were imprisoned at the same time. I can only imagine the fear of execution, but I pray that their faith and community gave them the strength to walk in His ways.

Proof things ruminate with us and you never know what will stick, another line that has stayed with me from a Jesuit priest years ago was "Who do you exclude?" To be in community is to inherently create an 'us' versus 'them.' Who does society exclude? Who do I exclude? These are things that have been percolating in my own brain for well over a decade by now.

December 30

Luke 2: 36-40

T here was a prophetess, Anna,
  the daughter of Phanuel, of the tribe of Asher.
She was advanced in years,
having lived seven years with her husband after her marriage,
and then as a widow until she was eighty-four.
She never left the temple,
but worshiped night and day with fasting and prayer.
And coming forward at that very time,
she gave thanks to God and spoke about the child
to all who were awaiting the redemption of Jerusalem.

When they had fulfilled all the prescriptions
of the law of the Lord,
they returned to Galilee,
to their own town of Nazareth.
The child grew and became strong, filled with wisdom;
and the favor of God was upon him.

St. Anysia

284-304

A nysia was born in the Early Church period, so what we know factually is limited. She is thought to have been born to a noble family in Thessalonica, Greece during the reign of Emperor Maximian Galerius. After the death of her parents she sold her possessions to distribute the money among the poor. She was one of the many hidden early Christians in Rome. Her name appears in the Roman Martyrology, the Greek Synaxary, and is mentioned by Early Church Fathers including the Patriarch of Constantinople of her time.

Anysia was traveling to an "assembly of the faithful," which was an underground or secret meeting of fellow believers for worship. While passing by one of the city gates, a guard was struck by her beauty. She tried to avoid his advances, but he was determined. The more she refused to acknowledge him or return his advances, the more agitated he became. She finally replied to his advances saying, "I am a servant of Jesus Christ and am going to the Lord's assembly." While trying to stop her, he ran his sword through her body, killing her on December 30, 303 (or 304). She is venerated in the Eastern Orthodox Church as well as the Roman Catholic Church.

It is always hard to know what is myth and what is fact with Early Church saints. Yet myths are used to teach us, and we can find kernels of facts within them. Anysia was a real woman, a martyr, and died due to her faith. Is her nobility important? Being an orphan? How does her identity as a woman fact in, especially one who refuses a man—specifically a man in power?

What can we learn from Anysia today?

Saint Anysia, help me to give to the Lord the glory due to him no matter the circumstance.

December 31

John 1: 1-17

In the beginning was the Word,
    and the Word was with God,
    and the Word was God.
He was in the beginning with God.
All things came to be through him,
    and without him nothing came to be.
What came to be through him was life,
    and this life was the light of the human race;
the light shines in the darkness,
    and the darkness has not overcome it.
A man named John was sent from God.
He came for testimony, to testify to the light,
so that all might believe through him.
He was not the light,
but came to testify to the light.
The true light, which enlightens everyone, was coming into the world.

He was in the world,
    and the world came to be through him,
    but the world did not know him.
He came to what was his own,
    but his own people did not accept him.
But to those who did accept him
   he gave power to become children of God,
   to those who believe in his name,
   who were born not by natural generation
   nor by human choice nor by a man's decision
   but of God.
And the Word became flesh
    and made his dwelling among us,
    and we saw his glory,
    the glory as of the Father's only-begotten Son,
    full of grace and truth
John testified to him and cried out, saying,
"This was he of whom I said,
'The one who is coming after me ranks ahead of me
because he existed before me.'"
From his fullness we have all received,
grace in place of grace,
because while the law was given through Moses,
grace and truth came through Jesus Christ.

St. Columba of Sens

257-273

C ompared to other early saints, even less is known about Columba. Butler lists her date of death as either 258 or 273. Her relics were kept in the Benedictine Abbey in France until the Huguenots dispersed them with other saints.

The Church's historical memory and tradition say Columba lived circa 256-273. Born in Spain, she died by beheading at Sens, France. She is the Patroness of rain and bears and you can see her as a Colonnade Saint at St. Peter's Square in Rome (no. 40 on the North Colonnade). We also know she was a popular saint during the Middle Ages. According to legend, she was born to a noble, pagan family in Spain. They fled to France, where Columba would later be baptized.

She would be arrested in Sens during the ongoing Christian persecution. She caught Emperor Aurelian's eye because of her beauty, so much so that he offered to have her marry his son. She was arrested when she refused. Because of this slight, she was thrown into a prostitution cell to be assaulted by Roman guards. When a guard entered, a she-bear appeared to protect her, causing him to run away and scare off any other guards who were sent in. When they tried to burn her alive, it rained.

Columba was eventually beheaded and buried in Sens by a man who recovered his sight after praying for her intercession. King Lothair III founded the Royal Abbey of Sainte-Columbe-Les-Sens on her tomb in 620. This tomb would be destroyed and rebuilt in 1164 and during the French Revolution until the Holy Childhood of Jesus and Mary purchased the land to keep the crypt safe. Columba's relics were transferred to the Cathedral of Sens in the ninth century, but numerous churches were dedicated to her in France, Spain, Germany, and Italy.

It is New Year's Eve. This season is an odd one with the beginning of the Catholic year at the beginning of Advent occurring while we wrap up the end of the calendar year. The short days seem to set the mood for introspection and looking ahead.

We once again have a saint from the early Church. St. Columba's legend has had more nuggets of information pass down than some of our other saints. Are any pieces of St. Columba's story speaking to you? While most of this may be legends, they have proven to be consistent. For example, I don't know why the gender of the bear is important but all sources I've read specified the bear to save her was female ("she-bear" appears in all my research— it is not my phrase).

What do you hope to achieve during the year? How do you hope to grow in your faith? What has reflecting on the Saints and Mary (over these past few days but also over the past year) shown you about yourself?

SAINT

ZDISLAVA
OF LEMBERK

January 1

Luke 2: 16-21

T he shepherds went in haste to Bethlehem and found Mary and Joseph,
and the infant lying in the manger.
When they saw this,
they made known the message
that had been told them about this child.
All who heard it were amazed
by what had been told them by the shepherds.
And Mary kept all these things,
reflecting on them in her heart.
Then the shepherds returned,
glorifying and praising God
for all they had heard and seen,
just as it had been told to them.

When eight days were completed for his circumcision,
he was named Jesus, the name given him by the angel
before he was conceived in the womb.

St. Zdîslava of Lemberk

1220-1252

Z dîslava was born circa 1220 in Moravia, which is modern-day Czech Republic. The Dominican Friars provide a short biography, highlighting that she was a mother and dedicated to the poor of her country. She received the Dominican habit and worked to build up the Dominican Order in the country with her husband before she died in 1252.

She was born into an aristocratic family and known to be rambunctious—she went off to live in the woods as a hermit at the age of seven. When she was older, she married the Count of Lemberk and had four children. She received Holy Communion daily, tended to the sick with her own hands, opened her home to the homeless, and experienced ecstasies and visions. One story tells of her husband becoming exasperated by her dedication to the poor that, when he heard she had given his bed to someone, he went in to evict the poor person. He was met with a cross instead and was converted to joining her in her work.

Zdîslava was canonized on May 21, 1995 by Pope St. John Paul II. He commented that she "is marked by an extraordinary capacity for self-giving." Pope Paul VI called her an example of "marital fidelity, a support of domestic spirituality and moral integrity." She is still remembered as a healer because of her generous efforts in charity, relief work, and bedside sickbed attendance. It was for the sick that she especially demonstrated such care and concern. Pope Saint John Paul II said "her example seems remarkably timely, particularly with regard to the value of the family, which—she teaches us—must be open to God, to the gift of life, and to the needs of the poor. Our saint is a marvelous witness to the 'Gospel of the family' and to the 'Gospel of Life.'"

Happy New Year! In addition to recognizing Saint Zdîslava it is also the Solemnity of the Blessed Virgin Mary, the Mother of God. While we reflect on Mary's role in salvation history, Zdîslava seems like another excellent woman to ponder. I'm going to state the obvious— no one is like Mary. To be in communion with God's will is an extraordinary gift. What I have enjoyed learning about all of these other women saints was how they, in their own ways, are offering their own gift for her Son.

Zdîslava's capacity for self-giving and domestic spirituality feels like gifts Mary would appreciate. To me, learning of St. Zdîslava's rambunctious childhood makes her relatable and I like to think Mary would appreciate the rambunctious young girl Zdîslava was. To me, it demonstrated a strength of character that saw her continue to live her life the best way she knew how and in the process brought her husband (and presumably her children) into active charity life.

Saint Zdîslava pray for us!

January 2

John 1: 19-28

This is the testimony of John.
When the Jews from Jerusalem sent priests and Levites to him
to ask him, "Who are you?"
he admitted and did not deny it, but admitted,
"I am not the Christ."
So they asked him,
"What are you then? Are you Elijah?"
And he said, "I am not."
"Are you the Prophet?"
He answered, "No."
So they said to him,
"Who are you, so we can give an answer to those who sent us?
What do you have to say for yourself?"
He said:
"I am *the voice of one crying out in the desert,*
'Make straight the way of the Lord,'
as Isaiah the prophet said."
Some Pharisees were also sent.
They asked him,
"Why then do you baptize
if you are not the Christ or Elijah or the Prophet?"
John answered them,
"I baptize with water;
but there is one among you whom you do not recognize,
the one who is coming after me,
whose sandal strap I am not worthy to untie."
This happened in Bethany across the Jordan,
where John was baptizing.

Bl. Odile Baumgarten & Bl. Marie-Anne Vaillot

1794

Odile Baumgarten sometimes written as Odile Baucard, was born in Gondrexange, France in 1750. She was the fourth child, but also the oldest (perhaps only) surviving child of a miller. At the age of 24, she became a postulant for the Daughters of Charity in Metz, the main city in the province of Lorraine. Her first appointment was to a hospital in Brest, but seven months after her arrival there the hospital was destroyed by fire. She was then transferred to St John's Hospital in Angers. She was put in charge of the pharmacy.

Marie-Anne Vaillot was born in Fontainebleau in 1734, the daughter of a stonemason. At the age of 27, she entered the Daughters of Charity in Paris. Her fourth appointment was to St John's Hospital in Angers where, presumably, she and Odile would meet.

The Daughters of Charity ran the hospital dedicated to St. John the Evangelist, the first hospital entrusted to their care. When the French Revolution broke out, it led to a lot of anti-religious sentiment and persecution. There was a lot of uncertainty over how nuns would be treated and what was expected of religious women who worked partly as State employees since the hospital received funding from the (recently deceased) monarch.

The anti-religious zeal led to the targeting of priests, and the Daughters of Charity eventually caught the attention of the community and government. The nuns were ordered to take the Oath of Liberty— an oath representing ideals meant to replace religion in the new French Republic— and to stop dressing in habits. Odile and Marie-Anne both refused to take the Oath. They, with a superior of their order, were arrested and questioned by the government. It is believed that the government decided to imprison the superior while Odile and Marie-Anne, identified as the troublemakers, were sentenced to execution by firing squad. By executing them it would set an example for the remaining nuns to comply with the Oath. They were bound together to walk to the field where the squad was executing prisoners. Odile was 46 years old. Marie-Anne was 60.

In total, 99 Martyrs from Angers are recognized by the Church. Odile and Marie-Anne are two of only three of the martyrs known by name.

At the risk of being repetitive, I cannot imagine being executed. Stories say Odilia leaned on Marie-Anne for strength; the fortitude it must have taken to walk to your own death!

Some of the other women witnessed great transformations during their lives. Odilia and Marie-Anne witnessed the chaos of the French Revolution and the Reign of Terror. To be strong in the face of such intensity (dare I say insanity) is a testament to their faith and their character. They are paired with the reading on John the Baptist, who was called to prepare the way for the Christ and who also would suffer a martyr's death for his beliefs. What can these religious sisters, friends, and martyrs show us today about living with our faith?

Blessed Odilia and Marie-Anne, I give thanks to God you had each other to strengthen your faith and resolve in the most dire of times. I pray for those who also face the most violent of persecutions because of their faith.

January 3

John 1: 29-34

John the Baptist saw Jesus coming toward him and said,
"Behold, the Lamb of God, who takes away the sin of the world.
He is the one of whom I said,
'A man is coming after me who ranks ahead of me
because he existed before me.'
I did not know him,
but the reason why I came baptizing with water
was that he might be made known to Israel."
John testified further, saying,
"I saw the Spirit come down like a dove from the sky
and remain upon him.
I did not know him,
but the one who sent me to baptize with water told me,
'On whomever you see the Spirit come down and remain,
he is the one who will baptize with the Holy Spirit.'
Now I have seen and testified that he is the Son of God."

St. Genevieve

Chief Patroness of Paris, 422-512

As another early saint, we once again have limited factual information to inform us about St. Genevieve. What we know comes from her relationship with male saints of her time. Genevieve is thought to be born in 422 to parents Severus and Gerontia, in a small village outside of Paris called Nanterre. When she was 7, the bishop, St. Germanus, was visiting the area and noticed Genevieve, declaring to her parents she would "perfectly accomplish the resolution she had taken of serving God." It is said that the young girl declared she wanted to serve God; Germanus told the family to meet him again the following morning and she, upon being questioned, remembered her vow from the previous night and still dedicated herself to God. Germanus gave her a brass medal with a cross as a reminder of her vows.

One version of Genevieve's story tells of her first miracle occurring when her mother struck her across the face; this caused her mother to lose her eyesight until she washed the mark with water Genevieve fetched and blessed with the Sign of the Cross.

At the age of 15, Genevieve entered religious life. Later in life, the Franks took over Gaul (present-day France) led by King Childeric. It was during his reign that a famine hit Paris. Genevieve led a group to secure provisions and returned to the city with boats of grain. This earned her the respect of King Childeric. Her numerous pilgrimages to the shrines of St. Martin of Tours and St. Dionysius led to Childeric's successor, King Clovis, to seek her advice.

When the Atilla the Hun prepared to attack Paris, Genevieve persuaded them not to abandon the city. She, with her religious sisters, led the city in acts of prayers and fasting, which are attributed to Atilla changing course. This may be where a popular devotion to St. Genevieve at St. John-le-Rond, the ancient public baptistery of the Church of Paris, first began.

St. Genevieve died on January 3, 512, and was buried near King Clovis, who died around the same time. Her remains were later enshrined near St. Owen in 630. She was buried with King Clovis and his wife, Queen Clotide, in *Abbey of Sainte-Geneviève* which was destroyed during the French Revolution. Today she is entombed in the St. Etienne du Mont Church.

What comes to mind reading Saint Genevieve's story paired with a reading on John the Baptist? I'm going to pause here and let you think for a moment.

For me, at least in this moment of my life, I find myself focused on her perseverance and leadership. Genevieve held steadfast to the idea of religious life and consecration to God throughout her childhood and maturing into adulthood. Part of me ponders on *how;* when I was a child "what I want to be when I grow up" changed several times. As I write this I realize that while the occupation changed, some things remained constant and one of those was how Mary gently placed an ember of devotion to her in my young heart (in a Protestant household no less!) and that only grew with time. While we don't have many facts of her childhood, we do know she was respected by the Kings of her day which, in my mind, makes me so curious about her!

Saint Genevieve, help me to grow in the face of life's challenges so that my faith and my self may be an example for those around me.

SAINT

ELIZABETH
ANN
SETON

January 4

John 1: 35-42

John was standing with two of his disciples,
and as he watched Jesus walk by, he said,
"Behold, the Lamb of God."
The two disciples heard what he said and followed Jesus.
Jesus turned and saw them following him and said to them,
"What are you looking for?"
They said to him, "Rabbi" (which translated means Teacher),
"where are you staying?"
He said to them, "Come, and you will see."
So they went and saw where he was staying,
and they stayed with him that day.
It was about four in the afternoon.
Andrew, the brother of Simon Peter,
was one of the two who heard John and followed Jesus.
He first found his own brother Simon and told him,
"We have found the Messiah," which is translated Christ.
Then he brought him to Jesus.
Jesus looked at him and said,
"You are Simon the son of John;
you will be called Cephas," which is translated Peter.

St. Elizabeth Ann Seton

1774-1821

K nown as the first American saint to be canonized, Elizabeth was born Elizabeth Ann Bayley in New York on August 28, 1774—two years before the signing of the Declaration of Independence. She was from a prominent, wealthy family of devout Episcopalians (Church of England). Her mother died when she was young, which affected her later in life, both when she became a mother and when she encountered the Blessed Virgin Mary.

At 19, she married a wealthy businessman, William Magee Seton, and they had five children. William contracted tuberculosis around the same time his business began to decline. In an attempt to improve his health, they traveled to Italy. Unfortunately, William died a few days after arrival. Widowed, with one of her daughters for company, Elizabeth remained in Italy with her late husband's business partners. Here, she was exposed to Catholicism. She was deeply moved by two main tenets—the Church's teachings on the Eucharist and the concept of Mary as mother to everyone. This perhaps spoke to the little girl she once was, who lost her own mother. When she returned to New York, she converted to the Catholic Church and took Mary as her baptismal name.

After several years of social discrimination and financial hardship, Elizabeth moved to Maryland in 1809. There she founded the Sisters of Charity of St. Joseph's, the first American community of religious sisters. She was elected to lead the community and became known as Mother Seton. She also established the St. Joseph's Academy and Free School, the first Catholic school in the country. She watched two of her daughters die of tuberculosis, and she also faced increasing health problems before she died on January 4, 1821, at 46 years old.

Although she died relatively young, her legacy continued. Today there are numerous congregations throughout the United States and Canada continuing her work. Mother Seton was canonized on September 14, 1975 by Pope Paul VI. Her remains are entombed in Emmitsburg in the Basilica at the National Shrine that bears her name.

For me, Elizabeth Ann Seton was the saint I knew the best when I started this project—yet I learned so much about her! Did anything speak to you? Coming back to this a year or so later, does something new speak to you? Two things struck me about Elizabeth Ann Seton. The first was her perseverance in overcoming loss after loss. The second was her devotion to Mary—it reminded me of what drew me to Mary as well.

Like the reading today where Peter faces his own transformation when joining Jesus, Mother Seton also had several pivotal moments that transformed her into the Saint she would become. Several of those moments were personal loss—her mother, her husband, her daughters. Somehow she not only continued on but established a legacy that has continued for over a century.

Have you experienced a similar loss? What grief have you experienced in your life? Even if it hasn't been from the loss of a loved one we have all been touched by grief. How has your faith helped you through that? Reading this year after year, how are you today?

January 5

John 1: 43-51

Jesus decided to go to Galilee, and he found Philip.
 And Jesus said to him, "Follow me."
Now Philip was from Bethsaida, the town of Andrew and Peter.
Philip found Nathanael and told him,
"We have found the one about whom Moses wrote in the law,
and also the prophets, Jesus, son of Joseph, from Nazareth."
But Nathanael said to him,
"Can anything good come from Nazareth?"
Philip said to him, "Come and see."
Jesus saw Nathanael coming toward him and said of him,
"Here is a true child of Israel.
There is no duplicity in him."
Nathanael said to him, "How do you know me?"
Jesus answered and said to him,
"Before Philip called you, I saw you under the fig tree."
Nathanael answered him,
"Rabbi, you are the Son of God; you are the King of Israel."
Jesus answered and said to him,
"Do you believe
because I told you that I saw you under the fig tree?
You will see greater things than this."
And he said to him, "Amen, amen, I say to you,
you will see the sky opened and the angels of God
ascending and descending on the Son of Man."

St Genoveva Torres Morales

1870-1956

Born on January 3, 1870, in Almenara Castille, Spain, Genoveva's early life was tragic. As the youngest of six children, by the time Genoveva was 8, her parents and all but one sibling had died. She was raised by her surviving brother, Jose. Because she didn't receive affection or companionship, she reverted to reading and solitude. By the age of 13, Genoveva had to have a leg amputated to prevent gangrene from spreading. This surgery was done at home with insufficient anesthesia; the surgery was excruciating and left her in pain for the rest of her life.

She lived at the Mercy Home run by the Carmelites of Charity for nine years, beginning around the age of fifteen. She deepened her spiritual life, piety, and perfected her sewing skills. Wanting to align herself with God's will and consecrate herself to God, she tried to join the Carmelites but was rejected, most likely due to her physical handicap. In 1894, determined to find a way to dedicate herself to God's will, Genoveva left the Carmelites and lived with two women who shared the solitude and liberty, supporting themselves with their sewing.

In 1911 Canon Barbarrós suggested Genoveva create a new religious community. It would fulfill her desire to consecrate her life to God and provide an opportunity to help the many poor women who could not afford to live on their own. This was a group in society Genoveva had often considered tending to since no one else was attending to the cares of poor, hardworking women. Thus the first community of the Congregation of the Sacred Heart of Jesus and the Holy Angels in Valencia was born; in 1953 they received Pontifical approval.

While Mother Genoveva was uncomfortable with the more public aspects of running a religious order, she dedicated the suffering to God. Following God's will led to true happiness, and Genoveva is known for her "spiritual liberty," renouncing everything that is not for the love of God and allowing God's freedom to exist through her.

Mother Genoveva died on January 5, 1956. She was known for her kindness, openness to all, and her sense of humor. She was canonized by Pope John Paul II on May 4, 2003. In his homily for the occasion, Pope Saint John Paul said Genoveva was "an instrument of God's tender love for lonely people in need of love, comfort and physical and spiritual care. The characteristic note that fueled her spirituality was adoration of the Eucharist for the expiation of sins, which formed the basis of an apostolate full of humility and simplicity, of self-denial and charity."

What stands out to you at the end of this Christmas season? New Year has come and gone, are you in the thick of the post-holiday craze? Still diligently following any resolutions?

For me, at this moment in time, the pairing with the reading of Nathaniel being called seems apropos! Genoveva had her own calling to Jesus. It took her longer to fulfill than she would have liked, I imagine, but she went with love and joy. Saint Genoveva, help me to find that love that leads to Spiritual Liberty.

What do you hope to bring with you into the New Year? Where do you hope to be, as a person, in your faith, when Christmas comes around again?

Acknowledgements

The amazing artists in this devotional

It took a village to bring this devotional to life, and I thank each of the ladies who contributed to this with their wonderful artwork! In order appearance:

Morning Star by Kristyn Brown, © TheSaintsProject.org

St. Anastasia ©Tracy L. Christianson, All Rights Reserved

St. Vincentia Maria Lopez Y Vicuna by Amanda Bergemen © This and That Publishing, LLC

St. Fabiola © Mindy Indy

St. Caterina Volpicelli by Yelhsa Art © This and That Publishing, LLC

The Martyrs of Seoul © Marina Baldwin

St. Anysia by Rebekah Balick reproduction © This and That Publishing, LLC

St. Columba of Sens © Amy Heyse

St. Zdislava of Lemberk © Theophilia Art

Sts. Odilia Baumgarten & Marie-Anne Vaillot © Kerri Bartee

St. Genevieve © Wagnon Studies/Jessie Wagnon

St. Elizabeth Ann Seton © Iconic Studio Art/Monica Sifert

St. Genoveva Torres Morales © Marybeth Foxhoven

A note on sources

The list of saints was compiled using Catholic Online (Catholic.org) calendar of Saint-of-the-Day. The site provides a brief overview of the saints. For more in-depth information, I also used a combination of the following sources:

Anderson, Ashlee. "Elizabeth Ann   Seton." *National Women's History Museum* www.womenshistory.org/students-and-educators/biographies/elizabeth-ann-seton

Baily Ogilvie, Marilyn. *Women in Science: Antiquity through the Nineteenth century A Biographical dictionary with Annotated Bibliography.* MIT Press.   1993 (fourth printing) for St. Fabiola

Butler, Alban. *Lives of the Saints*, vol IV, 59. Originally published 1903.

The   Catholic   Encyclopedia. New   York: Robert   Appleton   Company. www.newadvent.org

Congregation of the Mission of St. Vincent de Paul. www.svincent.og

Elizabeth Ann Seton Shrine. www.setonshrine.org

European Province of the Religious of Mary Immaculate. www.rmieuropa.com

Filles de la Charité de Saint Vincent de Paul. www.filles-de-la-charite.org

International   Catholic   Stewardship   Council   on   Fabiola.   at www.catholicstewardship.com

Letter   of   St   Jerome   on   Fabiola.   Translated   by   W.H.   Fremantle,   G. Lewis   and   W.G.   Martley. From Nicene   and   Post-Nicene   Fathers,   Second Series, Vol. 6. Edited by Philip Schaff and Henry Wace. (Buffalo, NY: Christian Literature Publishing Co., 1893.) Revised and edited for New Advent by Kevin Knight. http://www.newadvent.org/fathers/3001077.htm

the Vatican online archives at www.vatican.va

Vincentian Encyclopedia (for Odile and Marie-Anne) at wiki.famvin.org

Watkins, Basil. The Book of Saints: A Comprehensive Biographical Dictionary. 2016.

About the author

Christina Clare is a Catholic convert, cat mom, environmentalist, and nerd. She always joke she was "born Cradle Catholic but placed in the wrong cradle." She has a special devotion to Mary since she was a child--if accidently being named after 3 saints (by Protestant parents) wasn't enough of a sign of her impending conversion, her love for Mary certainly was! Her alter ego is a college professor where she has published on a variety of things, including Pope Francis. When not working or writing, you will probably find her reading or binge watching British murder mysteries.

You can follow Christina on facebook @Christina Clare, author or on her website www.christinaclare.com She promises not to spam you with newsletters but you can be the first to learn about upcoming projects in the "Mary and the Ladies" series.